Content

Arthur McBride	
Avondale	3
Band Played Waltzing Matilda, The	16
Black Velvet Band, The	8
Blackwater Side	56
Boston Burglar, The	22
Castle of Dromore, The	38
Cavan Girl	52
Danny Boy	24
Easy and Slow	4
Fiddler's Green	6
Galway Races, The	26
Humour is on me now, The	34
Little Old Mud Cabin on the Hill, The	36
Monto	10
Oró sé do Bheatha 'bhaile	28
Paddy's Green Shamrock Shore	42
Peggy Gordon	48
Raggle Taggle Gypsies	58
Ride On	32
Rocky Road to Dublin, The	62
Salonika	46
She Moved Through the Fair	60
Slieve Gallion Braes	40
Spancil Hill	14
St. Patrick was a Gentleman	54
Three Flowers, The	12
Three Lovely Lassies from Kimmage	50
Van Diemen's Land	44
Zoological Gardens, The	20

IRELAND THE SONGS VOLUME 1
ISBN 1 85720 059 4

Copyright © 1993 Walton Manufacturing Ltd.
2-5 North Frederick St., Dublin 1, Ireland,
Walton Music Inc., 110 Elm Street, Westfield, MA, 01085 U.S.A.
Printed in Ireland by Colour Books Ltd., Dublin

All photographs, including cover photograph © The Father Brown Collection.
All rights reserved. International copyright secured.

Sheep dipping in the Glen of the Downs, Co. Wicklow, 1932.

Avondale

Charles Parnell who dominated Irish politics at the end of the last century was born into the ascendancy. His family home was Avondale House in Co. Wicklow. The reaction of the Church to his affair with Kitty O'Shea, the wife of a British army officer, brought his political career to ruin.

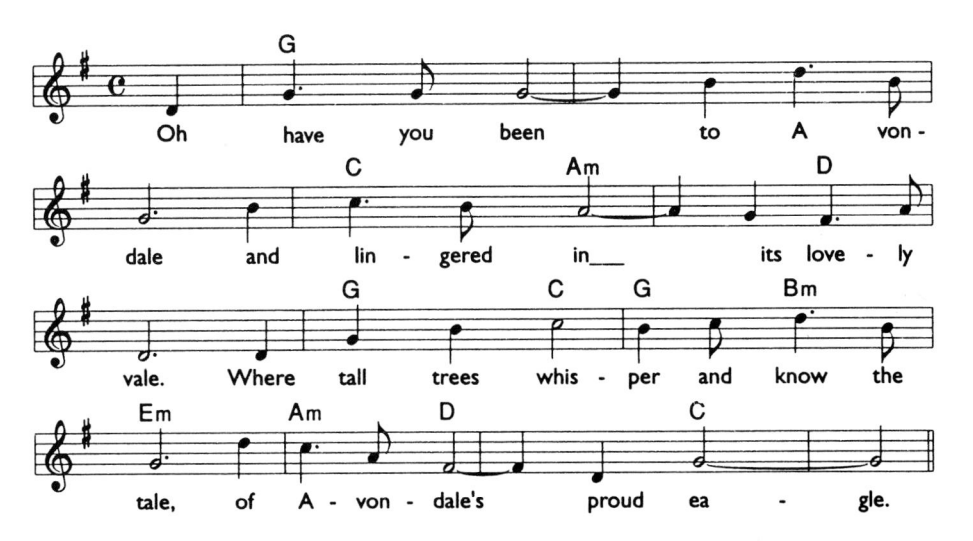

Oh have you been to Avondale and lingered in its lovely vale. Where tall trees whisper and know the tale, of Avondale's proud eagle.

Where pride and ancient glory fade,
So was the land where he was laid
Like Christ was thirty pieces paid
For Avondale's proud eagle.

Long years that green and lovely vale
Has nursed Parnell, her grandest Gael
And curse the land that has betrayed
Fair Avondale's proud eagle.

Easy and Slow

An old Dublin song, it was given new words by Seán O'Casey for his play "Red Roses for Me". It seems entirely appropriate that the character in the play who sings should be called "Brennan o' The Moor".

'Twas down by Christ-church that I first met with An-nie; a neat lit-tle girl and not a bit shy. She told me her fa-ther who came from Dun-gan-non, would take her back home in the sweet by and by. And what's it to a-ny man whe-ther or no, whe-ther I'm ea-sy or whe-ther I'm true, as she lif-ted her pet-ti-coat ea-sy and slow, and I tied up my sleeves for to buck-le her shoe.

We wandered by Thomas Street down to the Liffey
The sunshine was gone and the evening grew dark
Along by Kingsbridge and begod in a jiffy
Me arms were around her beyond in the park.
(CHORUS)

From city or country a girl is a jewel
And well made for gripping the most of them are
But any young man he is really a fool
If he tries at the first time to go a bit far.
(CHORUS)

Now if you should go to the town of Dungannon,
You can search till your eyes are weary or blind
Be you lying or walking or sitting or running
A girl like Annie, you never will find.
(CHORUS)

Fiddler's Green

The seaman's heaven. This song has the authentic atmosphere of a 19th century sea-song and while this version is by W. Connolly it bears much resemblance to an earlier song "Wrap Me Up In Me Tarpaulin Jacket."

As I walked by the dock-side one ev'-ning so fair___ To view the salt wa-ter and take the sea air.___ I heard an old fish-er-man sing-ing a song. Won't you take me a-way boys my time is not long___. Wrap me up in my oil-skins and jum-per___. No more on the docks I'll be seen___. Just tell my old ship-mates I'm tak-ing a trip mates and I'll see you one day in Fid-dl-er's green___ ___.

Now Fiddler's Green is a place I heard tell
Where fishermen go if they don't go to hell
Where the skies are all clear and the dolphins do play
And the cold coast of Greenland is far, far away.
(CHORUS)

When you get to the docks and the long trip is through
There's pubs, there's clubs and there's lassies there too,
Where the girls are all pretty and the beer it is free,
And there's bottles of rum growing from every tree.
(CHORUS)

Now I don't want a harp nor a halo, not me,
Just give me a breeze and a good rolling sea,
I'll play me old squeeze-box as we sail along
With the wind in the rigging to sing me a song.
(CHORUS)

Inscription on the Harper's Tombstone, Carrickmacross, Co. Monaghan, 1931.

Black Velvet Band

The places mentioned in this song suggest that it has crossed and re-crossed the Atlantic and changed in the process. What is not in doubt is the savagery of the penal code which allowed for transportation to Van Diemen's Land, now Tasmania, for what can only be regarded as petty crimes.

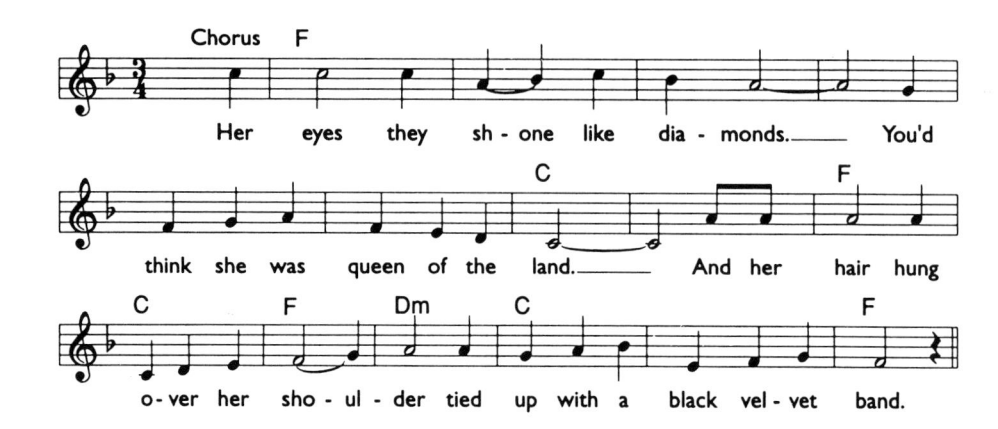

Chorus F

Her eyes they sh - one like dia - monds. You'd

C   F

think she was queen of the land. And her hair hung

C F Dm C   F

o - ver her sho - ul - der tied up with a black vel - vet band.

'Twas in the town of Tralee
an apprentice to trade I was bound
With a-plenty of bright amusement
to see the days go round
Till misfortune and trouble came over me,
which caused me to stray from my land,
Far away from my friends and relations,
to follow the Black Velvet Band.

As I went strolling down broadway
not intending to stay very long
I met with a frolicsome damsel
as she came tripping along.
A watch she took out of her pocket
and placed it right into my hand
On the very first day that I met her
Bad luck to her black velvet band.

Before the judge and the jury
the both of us had to appear,
And a gentleman swore to the jewellery
the case against us was clear,
For seven years transportation
right into Van Diemen's Land
Far away from my friends and relations,
to follow her Black Velvet Band.

Oh all you brave young Irish lads,
a warning take by me,
Beware of the pretty young damsels
that are knocking around in Tralee,
They'll treat you to whiskey and porter,
until you're unable to stand
And before you have time for to leave them,
you are unto Van Diemen's Land.

Monto

Refers to Montgomery Street north of Lower Abbey Street in the centre of Dublin. This was the heart of James Joyce's "Nighttown" in Ulysses. This huge red-light district with over 1600 "girls" which was closed almost overnight in 1925 is the subject of George Hodnett's song.

Well if you've got a wing-o, take her up to Ring-o, Where the wax-ies sing-o all the day. If you've had your fill of por-ter and you can't go an-y fur-ther, Give your man the or-der back to the quay. And take her up to Mon-to Mon-to Mon-to, Take her up to Mon-to Lan-ge-roo to you.

You've heard of Butcher Foster, the dirty old impostor,
He took a mot and lost her up the Furry Glen.
He first put on his bowler, then he buttoned up his trousers,
And he whistled for a growler and he said 'My man,
Take me up to Monto, Monto, Monto...

The fairy told him, 'Skin the goat'; O'Donnell put him on the boat,
He wished he'd never been afloat, the dirty skite.
It wasn't very sensible to tell on the Invincibles
They took aboard the principals, day and night
Be goin' up to Monto, Monto, Monto...

You've seen the Dublin Fusiliers, the dirty old bamboozaliers,
They went and got the childer, one, two, three.
Marchin' from the Linen Hall, there's one for every cannon ball
And Vicky's goin' to send you'se all o'er the sea.
But first go up to Monto, Monto, Monto...

When the Czar of Rooshia, and the King of Prooshia
Landed in the Phoenix in a big balloon,
They asked the Garda band to play The Wearin' O' The Green
But the buggers in the depot didn't know the tune,
So they both went up to Monto, Monto, Monto...

The queen she came to call on us, she wanted to see all of us,
I'm glad she didn't fall on us, she's eighteen stone.
'Mr Neill, Lord Mayor,' says she, 'Is this all you've got to show to me?'
'Why no, ma'am, there's some more to see póg mo thóin
And he took her up to Monto, Monto, Monto...
Took her up to Monto, langer oo.
Goodnight to you.

The Three Flowers

Norman G. Reddin wrote this fine song about three of the heroes of the 1798 period.

One time when walk-ing down a lane as night was draw-ing nigh, I met a col-leen with three flowers and she more young than I. "Saint Pat-rick bless you dear," I said, "If you'll be quick to tell the place where you did find those flowers I seem to know them well."

She took and kissed the first flower once,
And sweetly said to me:
'This flower comes from the Wicklow hills,
Dew wet and pure', said she,
'It's name is Michael Dwyer
The strongest flower of all;
But I'll keep it fresh beside my breast
Though all the world should fall.'

She took and kissed the next flower twice,
And sweetly said to me:
'This flower I culled in Antrim fields,
Outside Belfast,' said she.
'The name I call it is Wolfe Tone,
The bravest flower of all;
But I'll keep it fresh beside my breast
Though all the world should fall.'

She took and kissed the next flower thrice,
And softly said to me:
'This flower I found in Thomas street,
In Dublin fair.' said she.
'It's name is Robert Emmet,
The youngest flower of all;
But I'll keep it fresh beside my breast,
Though all the world should fall,
Then Emmet, Dwyer and Tone I'll keep,
For I do love them all;
And I'll keep them fresh beside my breast
Though all the world should fall.'

Spancil Hill

A Clare song about the emigrant's dream of home. Spancil Hill lies four miles from Ennis on the Tulla road and possesses no discernable hill.

Last night as I lay dreaming of pleasant days gone by, My mind being bent on rambling to Ireland I did fly, I stepped on board a vision and followed with a will, till I lately came to anchor at the cross near Spancil Hill.

Delighted by the novelty, enchanted with the scene,
Where in my early boyhood where often I had been
I thought I heard a murmur and I think I hear it still,
It's the little stream of water that flows down Spancil Hill.

It being the twenty-third of June, the day before the fair,
When Ireland's sons and daughters in crowds assembled there
The young, the old, the brave and the bold, they came for sport and kill
There were jovial conversations at the cross of Spancil Hill.

I paid a flying visit to my first and only love,
She's white as any lily and gentle as a dove
She threw her arms around me, saying "Johnny, I love you still"
She's Mag, the farmer's daughter and the pride of Spancil Hill.

I dreamt I stooped and kissed her as in the days of yore
She said "Johnny you're only joking, as many's time before"
The cock crew in the morning, he crew both loud and shrill,
And I woke in California, many miles from Spancil Hill.

"Which way to Killarney?", Molls Gap, December 1933.

The Band Played Waltzing Matilda

Eric Bogle is a living Australian song-writer with a rare talent for writing songs which seems to be woven into the fabric of the time when the events described in the song took place and yet makes a point with great relevance today.

When I was a young man I carried my pack. And I lived the free life of the rover. From the Murray's green basin to the dusty outback, I waltzed my Matilda all over. Then in nineteen fifteen my country said "Son it's time to stop rambling there's work to be done," So they gave me a tin hat, and they gave me a gun, and they sent me away to the war.

Chorus

And the band played Waltzing Matilda, As the ship pulled away from the quay, And amid all the cheers flag-waving and tears, we sailed off to Gallipoli.

How well I remember that terrible day
How the blood stained the sand and the water
And how in that Hell that they called Suvla Bay
We were butchered like lambs at the slaughter.
Johnny Turk he was ready, he primed himself well
He chased us with bullets, he rained us with shell
And in five minutes flat he'd blown us all to hell
Nearly blew us right back to Australia.
But the band played Waltzing Matilda
As we stopped to bury our slain
We buried ours and the Turks buried theirs
Then we started all over again.

Now, those that were left, well we tried to survive
In a mad world of blood, death and fire
And for ten weary weeks I kept myself alive
But around me corpses piled higher
Then a big Turkish shell knocked me arse over head

And when I woke up in my hospital bed
I saw what it had done and I wished I was dead
Never knew there were worse things than dying
For I'll go no more waltzing Matilda
All around the green bush far and near
For to hump tent and pegs, a man needs both legs
No more waltzing Matilda for me.

So they collected the cripples, the wounded, the maimed
And they shipped us back home, to Australia
The armless, the legless, the blind, the insane
Those proud wounded heroes of Suvla
And as our ship pulled into Circular Quay
I looked at the place my legs used to be
And thank Christ there was no one there waiting for me
To grieve and to mourn and to pity
And the band played Waltzing Matilda
As they carried us down the gangway
But nobody cheered, they just stood there and stared
Then turned all their faces away.

And now every April I sit on my porch
And I watch the parade pass before me
And I watch my old comrades, how proudly they march
Renewing old dreams of past glory
And the old men march slowly, all bent, stiff and sore
The tired old men from a forgotten war

And the young people ask,
"What are they marching for?"
And I ask myself the same question
And the band played Waltzing Matilda
And the old men still answer the call
But year after year their numbers get fewer
Some day no one will march there at all.

Last chorus, sung to the tune of 'Waltzing Matilda'

Waltzing Matilda, Waltzing Matilda
Who'll come a-waltzing Matilda with me
And their ghosts may be heard
as you pass the Billabong
Who'll come a-waltzing Matilda with me.

© Roberton Brown & Ass. This arrangement © 1993 Waltons Manufacturing Ltd.

The Zoological Gardens

This song, full of earthy humour comes from the Dublin of the late nineteenth century.

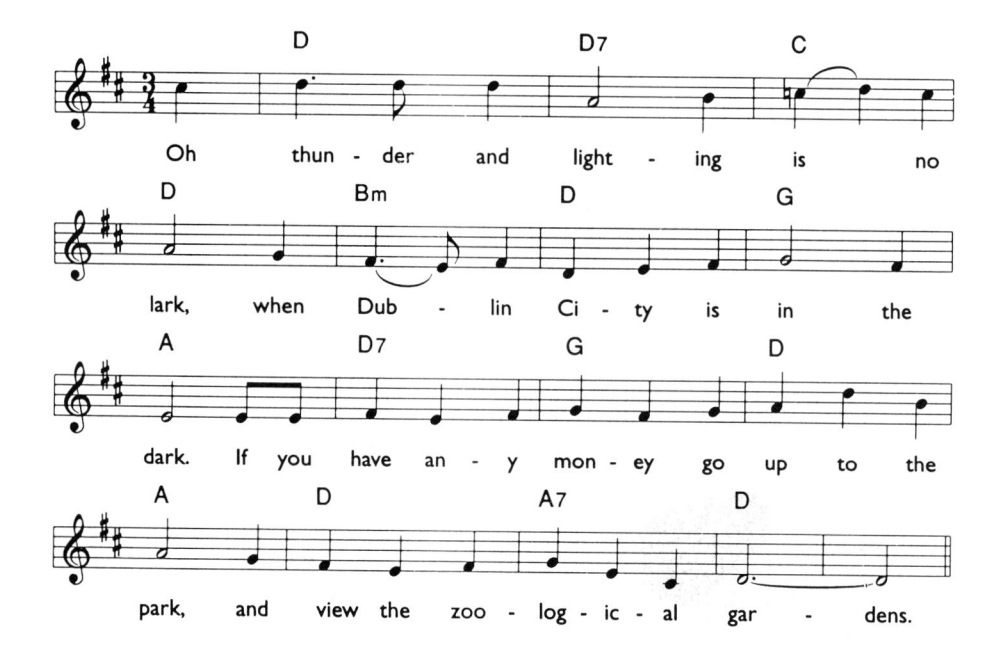

Oh thun-der and light-ing is no lark, when Dub-lin Ci-ty is in the dark. If you have an-y mon-ey go up to the park, and view the zoo-log-ic-al gar-dens.

Last Sunday night we had no dough
So I took the mot up to see the Zoo,
We saw the lions and the kangaroos,
Inside the Zoological Gardens.

Well we went out there by Castleknock
Said the mot to me "Sure we court by the Lough'
Then I knew she was one of the rare old stock,
Inside the Zoological Gardens.

Said the mot to me 'My dear friend Jack,
Sure I'd like a ride on the elephant's back'
'If you don't get out of that I'll give you such a crack'.
Inside the Zoological Gardens.

We went out there on our honeymoon,
Said the mot to me 'If you don't come soon,
I'll have to sleep with the hairy baboon,
Inside the Zoological Gardens.'

Carndonagh Fair, Co. Donegal, 1929.

The Boston Burglar

Sometimes called "Boston City". The geography of the events in this song would seem to suggest that it has been altered by crossing and re-crossing the Atlantic. While his crime was clearly committed in America the burglar vows that if he had his liberty he would "shun the robbing of the Munster Bank." Frank K. Brown, North California folklorist, identifies the song as an American version of the English ballad "Botany Bay".

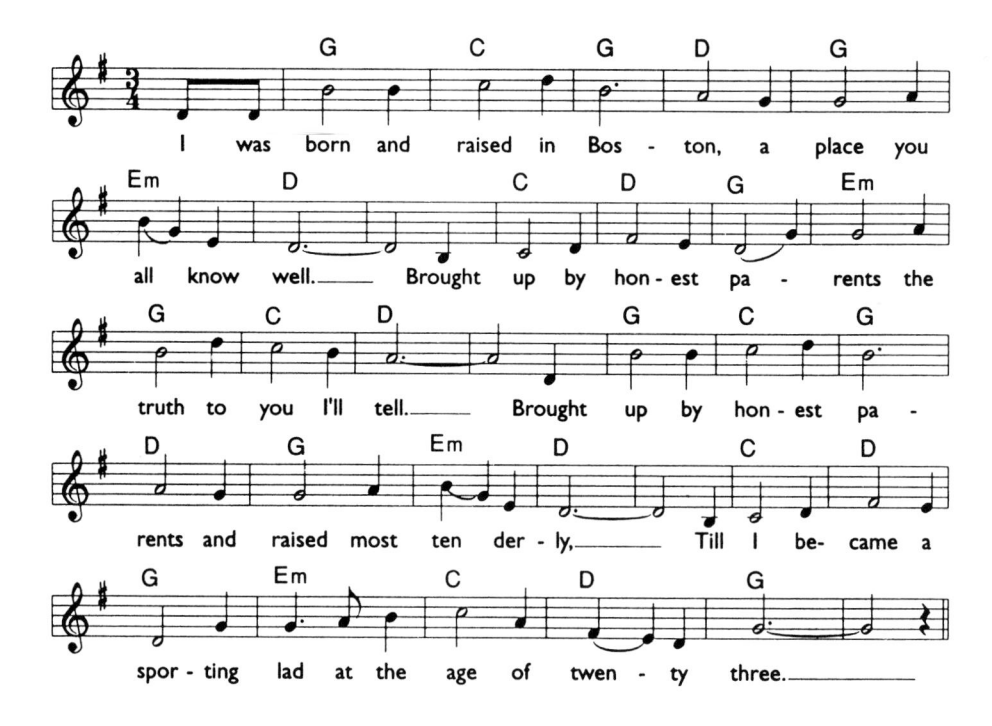

[Musical notation: I was born and raised in Boston, a place you all know well. Brought up by honest parents the truth to you I'll tell. Brought up by honest parents and raised most tenderly, Till I became a sporting lad at the age of twenty three.]

My character was taken and I was sent to jail
My parents thought to bail me out, but they found it all in vain;
The jury found me guilty, and the clerk he wrote it down
The judge he passed my sentence and I was sent to Charlestown.

I see my aged father and he standing by the Bar
Likewise my aged mother and she tearing out her hair
The tearing of her old grey locks
and the tears came tumbling down
Saying 'John, my son, what have you done,
that you're bound for Charlestown.

There's a girl in Boston city, boys,
a place you all know well
And if e'er I get my liberty, it's with her I will dwell
If e'er I get my liberty, bad company I will shun
The robbing of the Munster bank,
and the drinking of rum.

You lads that are at liberty, should keep it while you can
Don't roam the street by night or day,
or break the laws of man
For if you do you're sure to rue and become a lad like me
A-serving up your twenty-one years,
in the penitentiary.

Danny Boy

The air was collected in the 19th century by Jane Ross in Limavady, County Derry and published in the Petrie Collection. Rory Dall O'Cathain, chief harpist to Hugh O'Neill, is credited with composing the air. Of all the words which have been set to this air, those of Fred F. Weatherly, an Englishman, are the best known and most often sung.

Oh Danny Boy, the pipes the pipes are calling from glen to glen and down the mountainside. The summer's gone and all the flowers are dying, 'Tis you 'tis you must go and I must bide. But come you back when summer's in the meadow or when the

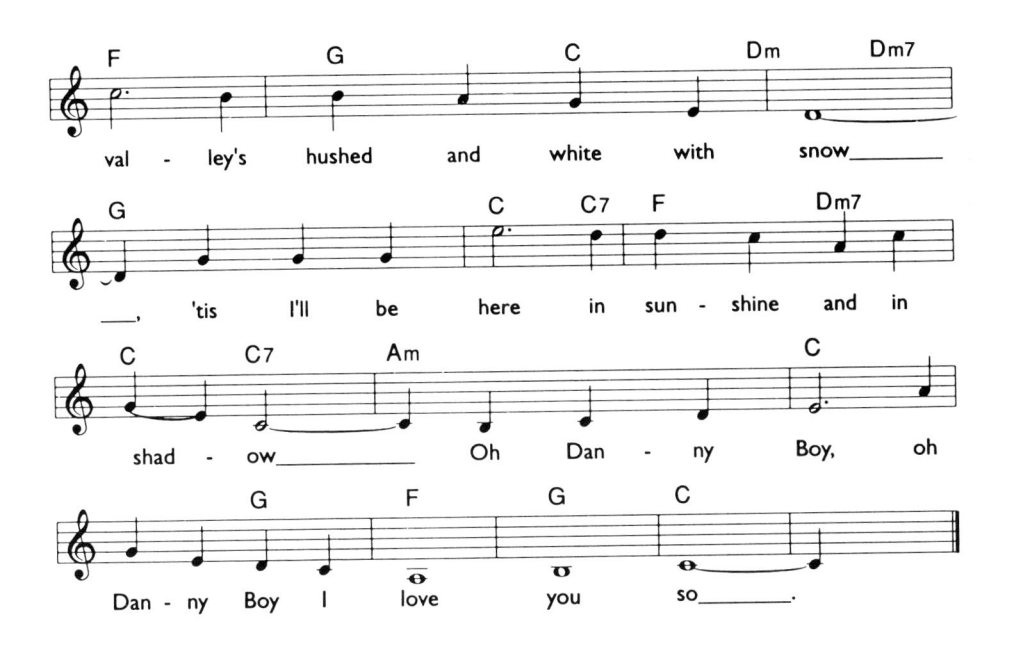

```
   F            G              C            Dm        Dm7
 val - ley's  hushed     and   white  with  snow_____

   G                      C    C7   F          Dm7
  ___, 'tis  I'll  be   here  in  sun - shine  and  in

   C     C7    Am                         C
  shad - ow_____       Oh   Dan - ny   Boy,      oh

         G      F        G       C
  Dan - ny  Boy  I    love    you    so_____.
```

And when you come and all the flowers are dying
If I am dead- as dead I well may be
You'll come and find a place where I am lying
And kneel and say an Ave there for me;
And I shall hear though soft your tread above me,
And all my grave shall warmer, sweeter be,
For you will bend and tell me that you love me
And I shall live in peace, until you come to me.

The Galway Races

This is an old tune with words from a 19th century balladsheet.

As I rode down to Galway town to seek for re-cre-a-tion on the seventeenth of August my mind was elevated, There were multitudes assembled with their tickets at the station. My eyes began to dazzle and them going to see the races. With me whack fol-de-da fol-de dith-er-y id-le day.

There were passengers from Limerick and passengers from Nenagh
And passengers from Dublin and sportsmen from Tipp'rary
There were passengers from Kerry and all the quarters of the nation
And our member, Mr Hasset for to join the Galway Blazers.

There were multitudes from Aran and members from New Quay Shore
The boys from Connemara and the Clare unmarried maidens
There were people from Cork city who were loyal, true and faithful
That brought home the Fenian prisoners from dying in foreign nations.

It's there you'll see confectioners with sugarsticks and dainties
The lozenges and oranges, the lemonade and raisins
The gingerbread and spices to accommodate the ladies
And a big crubeen for three pence to be picking while you're able.

It's there you'll see the gamblers, the thimbles and the garters
And the sporting Wheel of Fortune with the four and twenty quarters
There were others without scruple pelting wattles at poor Maggy
And her father well contented and he looking at his daughter.

It's there you'll see the pipers and the fiddlers competing
And the nimble-footed dancers and they tripping on the daisies
There were others crying 'Cigars and lights and bills of all the races
With the colours of the jockeys and the prize and horses' ages'.

It's there you'd see the jockeys and they mounted on most stately
The pink and blue, the red and green, the emblem of our nation
When the bell was rung for starting all the horses seemed impatient
I thought they never stood on ground, their speed was so amazing.

There was half a million people there of all denominations
The Catholic, the Protestant, the Jew and Presbyterian
There was yet no animosity, no matter what persuasion
But fáilte and hospitality inducing fresh acquaintance.

Óró 'Sé Do Bheatha 'Bhaile

Padraig Pearse one of the leaders of the 1916 rising wrote this song as an impassioned plea to all Irishmen fighting for Britain in Europe to return and lend a hand to the great struggle for freedom at home.

'Sé do bhea - tha 'bhean ba léan - mhar b'é ár greach tú bheith i ngéibh - eann. Do dhúi - che bhreá i - sei - lbh méir - leach 'stú díol - ta leis na Gall - aibh. Ó - ró 'sé do bhea - tha 'bhai - le ór - ro 'sé do bhea - tha 'bhai - le Ó - ró 'sé do bhea - tha 'bhai - le 'Nois ar theacht an tsamh - raidh.

Tá Gráinne Mhaol ag teacht thar sáile;
Óglaigh armtha léi mar gharda
Gaeil iad féin is ní Gaill ná Spáinnigh;
Is cuirfidh siad ruaig ar Ghallaidh
(CHORUS)

A bhuí le Rí na bhfeart go bhfeiceam;
Muna mbíom beo ina dheoidh ach seachtain
Gráinne Mhaol is míle gaiscíoch;
Ag fógairt fáin ar Ghallaibh.
(CHORUS)

"The Thatcher" at Ashford, Co. Wicklow, 1932.

Arthur McBride

The best of the anti-recruiting songs, it comes from the late 18th century. It was collected in several places, Limerick by Patrick Joyce, Donegal by Petrie and in Scotland and England. Paul Brady brought back a version from America.

I had a first cous-in called Ar-thur Mc Bride. He and I took a stroll down by the sea-side, a seek-ing good for-tune and what might be-tide being just as the day was a-dawn-ing. Then af-ter rest-ing we both took a tramp, we met Ser-geant Har-per and Cor-por-al Cramp, be-sides the wee drum-mer who beat up for camp with his row-dy dow dow in the morn-ing.

He says 'My young fellow, if you will enlist
A Guinea you quickly shall have in your fist
Besides a Crown for to kick up the dust
And drink the King's health in the morning
Had we been such fools as to take the advance
For the wee bit of money we'd have to run chance
For you'd think it no scruples to send us to France
Where we would be killed in the morning

He says 'My young fellows, if I hear but one word
I instantly now will out with my sword
And into your bodies as strength will afford
So now, my gay devils take warning'.
But Arthur and I we took in the odds
We gave them no chance to launch out their swords
Our whacking shillelaghs came over their heads
And paid them right smart in the morning.

As for the wee drummer; we rifled his pouch
And we made a football of his rowdy-dow-dow
And into the ocean to rock and to row
And barring the day its returning.
As for the old rapier that hung by his side
We flung it as far as we could in the tide
'To the devil I bid you' says Arthur McBride
To temper your steel in the morning.

Ride On

Another fine song from Jimmy McCarthy of Cork.

(Verse 1 with melody)

True you ride the fi-nest horse I'v ev-er seen
stand-ing six-teen one or two, with
eyes wide and green. And you ride the
horse so well. Hands light to the touch
I could ne-ver go with you no mat-ter how I want-ed to.

Chorus
Ride, on, see you, I could ne-ver
go with you no mat-ter how I want-ed to.

When you ride into the night without a trace behind,
Run your claw along my gut one last time;
I turn to face an empty space where once you used to lie
And look for a smile to light the night through a teardrop in my eye.
(CHORUS)

© M.C.P.S. This arrangement © 1993 Walton Manufacturing Ltd.

"The Candyman" at Dundalk, Co. Louth, 1928.

The Humour is on Me Now

This humourous look at the trial of marriage was closely associated with Delia Murphy, a famous ballad singer back in the fifties before that title acquired the meaning it has has had in recent years.

[Sheet music with lyrics:]
As I went out one morning it being the month of May, A farmer and his daughter I spied upon my way, and the girl sat down quite calmly to the milking of her cow, Saying I will and I must get married for the humour is on me now

Ah, be quiet you foolish daughter and hold your simple tongue,
You're better free and single and happy while you're young
But the daughter shook her shoulders and milked her patient cow
Saying "I will and I must get married for the humour is on me now"

And, sure who are you to turn me, that married young yourself,
And took my darling mother from off the single shelf?
Ah, sure, daughter dear go aisy and milk your patient cow
For a man may have his humour but the humour is off me now,

Well indeed, I'll tell my mother the awful things you say,
Indeed I'll tell my mother this very blessed day;
Och, now, daughter have a heart, dear, you'll start a fearful row,
So I will unless I marry for the humour is on me now.

Och, if you must be married will you tell me who's the man?
And quickly she did answer there's William, James and John,
A carpenter, a tailor and a man to milk the cow,
For I will and I must get married and the humour is on me now.

A carpenter's a sharp man, and a tailor's hard to face,
With his legs across the table and his threads about the place,
And sure John's a fearful tyrant and never lacks a row-
But I will and I must get married for the humour is on me now.

Well if you must be married will you tell me what you'll do?
"Sure I will" the daughter answered, "Just the same as ma and you"
"I'll be mistress of my dairy and my butter and my cow,"
"And your husband too, I'll venture, for the humour is on me now".

So, at last the daughter married and married well-to-do,
And loved her darling husband for a month, a year or two;
But John was all a tyrant and she quickly rued her vow
Saying "I'm sorry that I married for the humour is OFF me now"

The Little Old Mud Cabin On The Hill

Written by the much loved radio presenter Leo Maguire who for many years exhorted the nation with the Walton's Message, "And if you feel like singing, do sing an Irish song."

Go sell the pig and cow a ghrá to take you far away. For your poor parents you must leave behind. Go seek your fortune darling in the land beyond the sea. For in Paddy's land 'tis poverty you'll find. Those were the words my father said when I left old Ireland's shore. And his sad farewell is in my mem'ry

...still. So I packed my bundle on my back and left for ever more, the little old mud cabin on the hill.

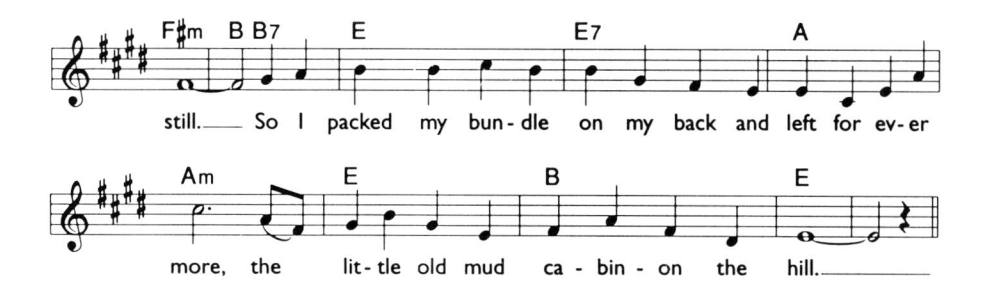

The roof is thatched with straw,
the walls are white as snow,
And the turf fire boils the pot- I see it still,
For old Ireland's graven on my heart,
the place where I was born,
In that little old mud cabin on the hill.

I think I see the turf fire, it attracts my father's gaze,
And my dear old mother sitting by his side;
His pipe is lit, the smoke ascends, he's thinking of the time
That took his darling boy beyond the tide.
No more I'll join the merry dance upon the cabin floor,
To music of the bagpipes loud and shrill,
No more I'll see those happy times I spent in days of yore
In that little old mud cabin on the hill.
Chorus

The Castle of Dromore

The Castle of Dromore on the Ring of Kerry is sited on the banks of the river Blackwater. All the ingredients of a lullaby are woven into a gentle poem set to an old traditional air.

Oc - to - ber winds la - ment a - round the Cas - tle of Dro - more.— Yet peace is in it's lof - ty halls a pháis - te bán a stór.— Though aut - umn leaves may droop and die, a bud of spring are you. Sing hush - a - bye lú - ló - lú ló - lan sing hush - a - bye lú - ló - lú.—

Bring no ill wind to hinder us,
my helpless babe and me-
Dread spirit of Blackwater banks,
Clan Eoin's wild banshee,
And Holy Mary pitying us,
in heaven for grace doth sue,
Sing Hushabye, lú, ló, lú, ló, lan
Sing hushabye, lú, ló, lú.

Take time to thrive, my ray of hope,
in the garden of Dromore;
Take heed young Eagle - till your wings
are feathered fit to soar;
A little rest and then our land
is full of things to do.
Sing Hushabye, lú, ló, lú, ló, lan
Sing hushabye, lú, ló, lú.

Handball played against the Castle wall at Ferns, Co. Wexford, 1930.

Slieve Gallion Braes

Evictions of tenant farmers by landlords constantly raising rents right through the nineteenth century caused many to emigrate. The braes in question are in the Sperrin mountains straddling counties Tyrone and Derry.

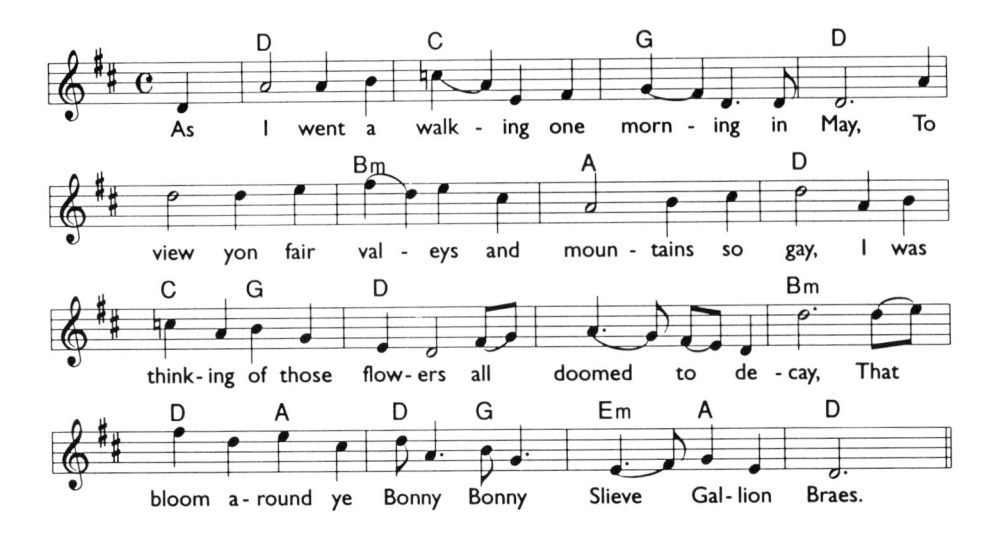

As I went a walking one morning in May, To view yon fair valleys and mountains so gay, I was thinking of those flowers all doomed to decay, That bloom around ye Bonny Bonny Slieve Gallion Braes.

How oft in the morning with my dog and my gun
I roam through the glens for joy and for fun
But those days are now all over and I must go away
So farewell unto ye, bonny, bonny, Slieve Gallion Braes.

How oft of an evening and the sun in the West
I roved hand in hand with the one I loved best
But the hopes of youth are vanished and now I'm far away
So farewell unto ye, bonny, bonny, Slieve Gallion Braes.

It's not for the want of employment at home
That caused us poor exiles in sorrow to roam
But those tyrannising landlords, they would not let us stay
So farewell unto ye, bonny, bonny, Slieve Gallion Braes.

Ballaghbeama Gap, Co. Kerry, 1926

Paddy's Green Shamrock Shore

This song appears in "A Collection of Songs and Shanties" by Joseph Rawles (1948). There is some geographical confusion in the song mixing Botany Bay with New York but this could be a result of the song having travelled a lot with singing sailors.

Oh fare-thee well to Ireland, my own dear native land___, It breaks my heart to see friends part. Fot it's then that the tear drops fall___, I'm on my way to America, Will I ever see home once more?___, For now I leave my own true love, And Paddy's Green Shamrock Shore___.

From Derry quay we sailed away,
it being on the fourth of May.
Pleasant weather I'm sure we had going to America.
Fresh water then we did take in,
one hundred tons or more
For fear we'd be short on the other side,
far from the Shamrock shore.

Two of our anchors we did weigh
before we left the quay;
Down the river we were towed till we came to Botany Bay.
We saw that night the grandest night
we ever saw before,
The sun's going down 'tween sea and sky
far from the Shamrock shore.

Early next morning we were sea-sick all,
not one of us was free.
I, myself was confined to bed with no one to pity me;
No father or no mother
to raise my head when sore;
That made me think of the friends
I left on the lonely Shamrock shore.

We landed safely in New-York after four and twenty days,
Each comrade by the hand we took
and we marched through different ways.
Each one drank a flowing glass
as we might meet no more.
With flowing bumpers we drank a health
to the lonely Shamrock shore.

Van Diemen's Land

In the 18th and 19th century deportation to Australia was the penalty for even petty crime and many thousands of Irish suffered that fate. This ballad first appeared on a broadsheet in 1830.

Come all you gallant poachers that ramble void of care. That walk out on a moonlit night with your dog and gun and snare. The hare and lofty pheasant you have at your command. Not thinking of your last career upon Van Diemen's land.

Poor Thomas Brown from Nenagh town, Jack Murphy and poor Joe
Were three determined poachers as the county well does know,
By the keepers of the land, my boys, one night they were trepanned
And for fourteen years transported unto Van Diemen's Land.

The first day that we landed upon that fatal shore
The planters came around us, there might be twenty-score
They ranked us off like horses and they sold us out of hand
And they yoked us to the plough, brave boys, to plough
Van Diemen's Land.

The cottages we live in are built with sods of clay
We have rotten straw for bedding but we dare not say nay
Our cots we fence with firing and slumber when we can
To keep the wolves and tigers from us in Van Diemen's Land.

Oft times when I do slumber I have a pleasant dream
With my sweet girl sitting near me close to a purling stream
I am roaming through old Ireland with my true love by the hand
But awaken broken-hearted upon Van Diemen's Land.

God bless our wives and families, likewise that happy shore
That isle of sweet contentment which we ne'er shall see more
As for the wretched families, see them we seldom can
There are twenty men for one woman in Van Diemen's Land.

But fourteen years is a long time, that is our fatal doom
For nothing else but poaching for that is all we done
You would leave off both dog and gun and poaching, every man,
If you but knew the hardship that's Van Diemen's Land.

Oh if I had a thousand pounds all laid out in my hand
I'd give it all for liberty if that I could command
Again to Ireland I'd return and be a happy man
And bid adieu to poaching and to Van Diemen's Land.

Salonika

This town in Greece was the scene of a battle in the First World War when the Munster Fusiliers took on the Turks. A "slacker" was a man who did not join and stayed at home.

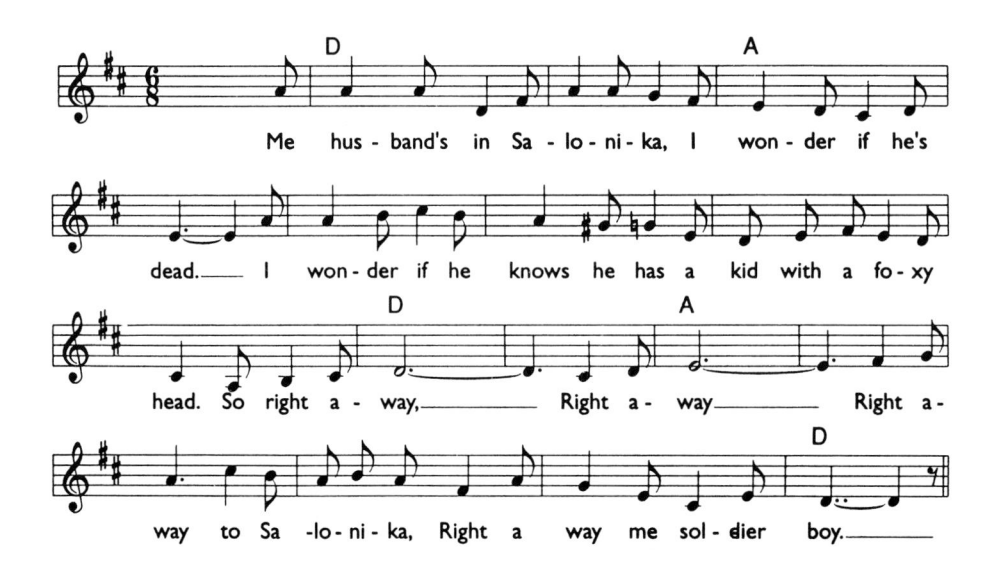

Me hus-band's in Sa-lo-ni-ka, I won-der if he's dead. I won-der if he knows he has a kid with a fo-xy head. So right a-way, Right a-way Right a-way to Sa-lo-ni-ka, Right a way me sol-dier boy.

Now when the war is over what will the slackers do ?
They'll be all around the soldiers for the loan of a bob or two
So right away etc.

Now when the war is over what will the soldiers do?
They'll be walking around on a leg and a half and the slackers they'll have two
So right away etc.

They taxed our pound of butter,
they taxed our half penny bun
But still with all their taxes, they can't bate the bloody Hun.
So right away etc.

They taxed the Coliseum, they taxed St. Mary's Hall
Why don't they tax the Bobbies
with their backs against the wall.
So right away etc.

Now when the war is over what will the slackers do
For every kid in America in Cork there will be two.
So right away etc.

They take us out to Blarney and lays us on the grass
They puts us in the family way and leaves us on our ass.
So right away etc.

There's lino on the Parlour and in the kitchen too
There's a glass back chevonier
that we got from Dicky Glue.
So right away etc.

Now never marry a soldier, a sailor or a marine
Now keep you eyes on the Sinn Féin Boy
with his yellow, white and green.
So right away etc.

Peggy Gordon

Another song brought to Ireland by Luke Kelly, this time from Scotland. Luke's artistry was such that he made songs like this seem indispensable parts of the Irish ballad singer's repertoire.

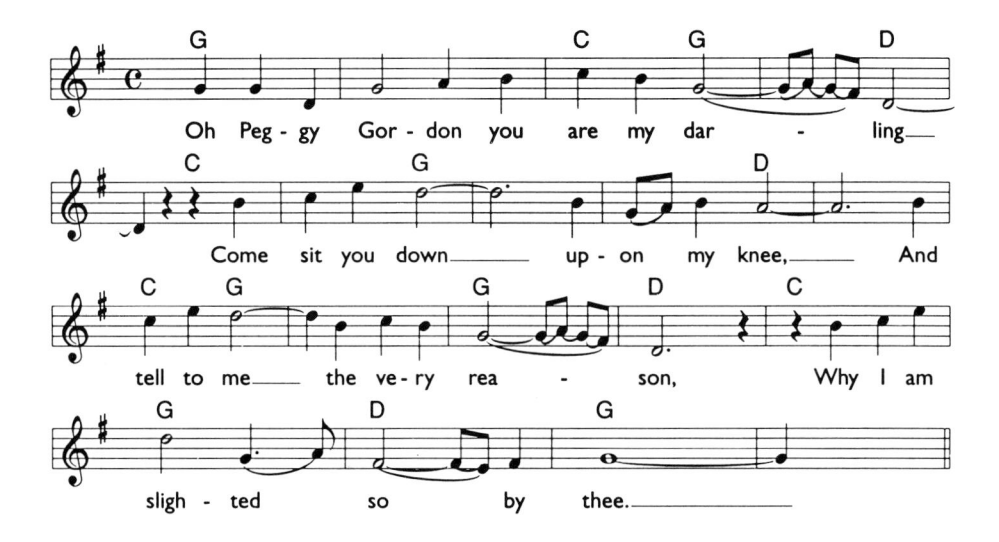

Oh Peg-gy Gor-don you are my dar-ling, Come sit you down up-on my knee, And tell to me the ve-ry rea-son, Why I am sligh-ted so by thee.

I wish I was in some lonesome valley,
Where womankind cannot be found,
Where the little birds sing upon the branches,
And every moment a different sound.

I'm so in love that I can't deny it,
My heart lies smothered in my breast,
But it's not for you to let the world know it,
A troubled mind can know no rest.

I put my head to a cask brandy,
It was my fancy, I do declare,
For when I'm drinking I'm always thinking,
And wishing Peggy Gordon was here.

I wish I was away in England,
Far across the briny sea,
Or sailing o'er the deepest ocean,
Where care and troubles can't bother me.

Repeat first verse.

"A Mountain Home", Ballingeary, Co. Cork, 1926.

Three Lovely Lassies from Kimmage

A Dublin version of the song "Three Lovely Lassies from Banion". Dubliners of the appropriate age will well remember the Adelaide Hall as a great venue for dancing in the fifties.

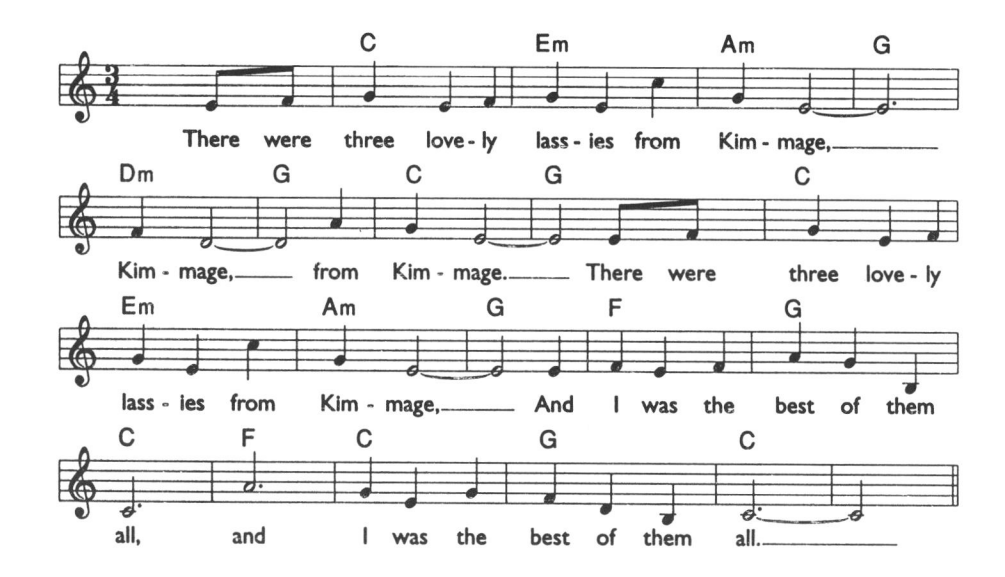

There were three love-ly lass-ies from Kim-mage, Kim-mage, from Kim-mage. There were three love-ly lass-ies from Kim-mage, And I was the best of them all, and I was the best of them all.

Well the cause of the row is Joe Cashin,
Joe Cashin, Joe Cashin, Joe Cashin,
For he told me he thought I looked smashin'
At a dance at the Adelaide Hall,
At a dance at the Adelaide Hall.

He told me he thought we should marry,
Should marry, should marry, should marry,
He said it was foolish to tarry,
So he lent me the price of a ring,
So he lent me the price of a ring.

When he gets a few jars he goes frantic,
Goes frantic, goes frantic, goes frantic,
Well he's tall and he's dark and romantic,
And I love him in spite of it all,
And I love him in spite of it all.

Well me dad said he'd give us a present,
A present, a present, a present,
A stool and a lovely stuffed pheasant,
And a picture to hang on the wall,
And a picture to hang on the wall.

I went down to the tenancy section,
The section, the section, the section,
The T.D. just before the election,
Said he'd get me a house near me ma,
Said he'd get me a house near me ma.

Well I'm getting a house the man said it,
Man said it, man said it, man said it,
When I've five or six kids to me credit,
In the meantime we'll live with me ma,
In the meantime we'll live with me ma.

Cavan Girl

Thom Moore, an American who periodically lives in Ireland and was a member of the bands 'Pumpkinhead' and 'Midnight Well', wrote this song for the Cavan Song Contest and won.

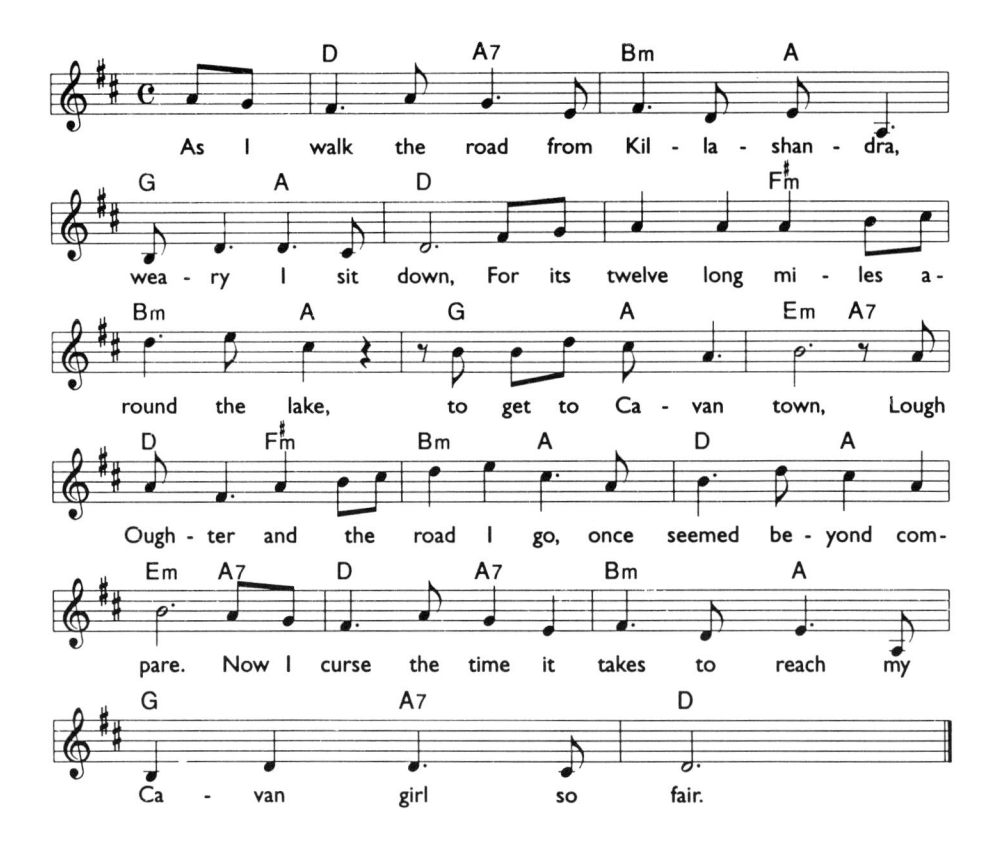

As I walk the road from Kil-la-shan-dra,
wea-ry I sit down, For its twelve long mi-les a-
round the lake, to get to Ca-van town, Lough
Ough-ter and the road I go, once seemed be-yond com-
pare. Now I curse the time it takes to reach my
Ca-van girl so fair.

The autumn shades are on the leaves, the trees will soon be bare
And each red coat leaf around me seems, the colour of her hair
My gaze retreats defies my feet and once again I sigh
For a broken pool of sky reminds; The colour of her eyes.

© M.C.P.S. This arrangement © 1993 Waltons Manufacturing Ltd.

At the Cavan cross each Sunday morning, it's there she can be found
And she seems to have the eye of every boy in Cavan town
If my luck will hold I'll have the golden summer of her smile
And to break the hearts of Cavan men she'll talk to me a while.

So next Sunday evening finds me homeward Killashandra bound
To work a week till I return to court in Cavan town
When asked if she would be my bride at least she'd not said no
So next Sunday morning 'rouse myself and back to her I go.

Donard, Co. Wicklow, 1929.

St. Patrick was a Gentleman

A music hall song re-popularised by Christy Moore.

Saint Patrick was a gentleman, he came from decent people. In Dublin town he built a church and on it put a steeple. His father was a Callahan his mother was a Grady, His aunt was an O'Shaughnessy, and his uncle was a Brady. Then success to bold St. Patrick's fist. He was a saint so clever. He gave the snakes an awful twist and banished them for ever.

There's not a smile in Ireland's Isle
where the dirty vermin musters,
Where'er he put his dear forefoot
he murder'd them in clusters.
The toads went hop, the frogs went plop,
slap dash into the water,
And the beasts committed suicide
to save themselves from slaughter.
(CHORUS)

Nine hundred thousand vipers blue
he charm'd with sweet discourses,
And dined on them at Killaloo
in soups and second courses.
When blind worms crawling on the grass
disgusted all the nation,
He gave them a rise and open'd their eyes
to a sense of their situation.
(CHORUS)

The Wicklow hills are very high,
and so's the hill of Howth, sir,
But there's a hill much higher still,
Ay, higher than them both, sir.
'Twas on the top of his hill
St. Patrick preach'd the "sarmint,"
That drove the frogs into the bogs,
and bothered all the "varmint."
(CHORUS)

Blackwater Side

The banks of the Blackwater river in Cork is the scene of this seduction and betrayal. Seldom has this universal theme been treated with more heartaching beauty, especially in a version by Liam Clancy.

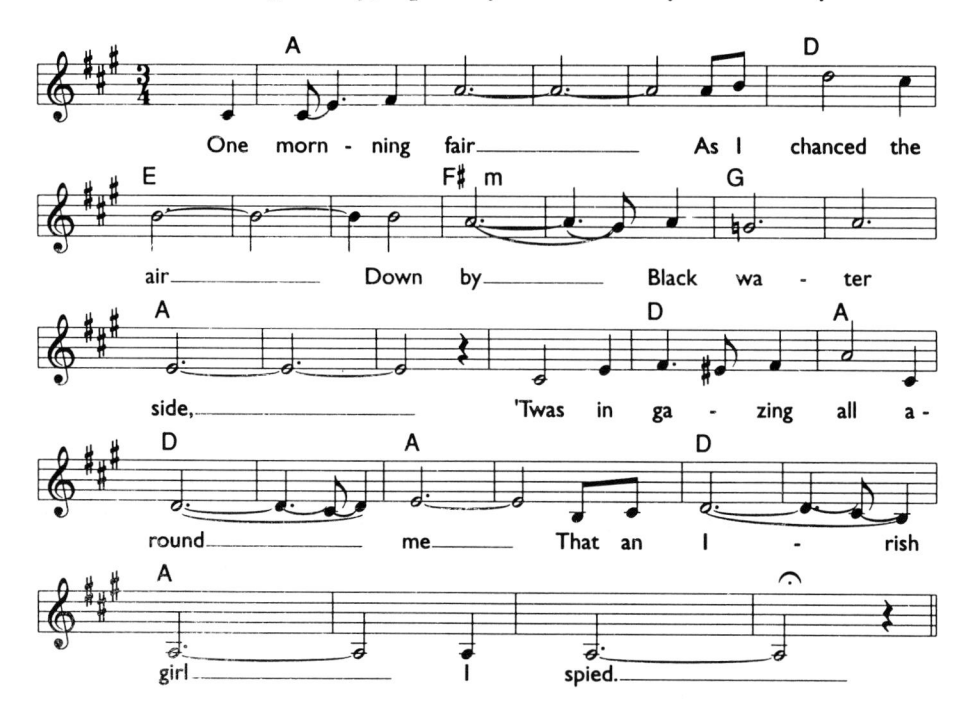

One morning fair, As I chanced the air, Down by Blackwater side, 'Twas in gazing all around me That an Irish girl I spied.

"All in the fore part of the night
They rolled in sport and play,
Then this young man arose and he put on his clothes,
Saying "Far thee well today."

"That's not the promise you made to me
When you lay upon my breast;
You could make me believe with your lying tongue
That the sun rose in the West.

"Go home, go home to your father's garden,
Go home and cry your fill;
And think of the sad misfortune
I brought on with my wanton will."

"There's not a flower in this whole world
As easily led as I;
And when fishes can fly and seas do run dry,
It is then that you'll marry I."

Sand-diggers on the Liffey near Lucan, Co. Dublin, 1925.

Raggle Taggle Gypsies

The song 'The Whistling Gypsy" by Leo Maguire is an updated version of this song. The original was Scottish and was based on the execution in 1624 of Johnny Faa, a Scottish Gypsy Chieftain. The lady was regained by her husband. This seems to have been too unromantic for all later versions which have the lady happily taking off with the Gypsies, never to return.

There were three gyp-sies came to our hall door, and down-stairs ran this la-dy-o, There was one sang high, and the oth-er sang low, and the oth-er sang Bon-ny Bon-ny Bis-cay-o.

They sang so sweet, they sang so shrill,
That fast her tears began to flow
And she laid down her silken gown
Her golden rings and all her show.

She plucked off her high-heeled shoes,
A-made of Spanish leather, O
She went in the street with her bare, bare feet;
All out in the wind and weather, O.

O saddle to me my milkwhite steed,
And go and fetch my pony, O
That I may ride and seek my bride,
Who is gone with the raggle taggle gypsies, O.

O he rode high and he rode low,
He rode through wood and copses too,
Until he came to an open field,
And there he espied his lady, O.

What makes you leave your house and land
Your golden treasures for to go
What makes you leave your new-wedded lord,
To follow the raggle taggle gypsies, O.

What care I for my house and my land
What care I for my treasure, O
What care I for my newly-wedded lord,
I'm off with the raggle taggle gypsies, O.

Last night you slept on a goose-feather bed,
With the sheets turned down so bravely, O
And to-night you'll sleep in a cold open field,
Along with the raggle taggle gypsies, O.

What care I for a goose-feather bed
With the sheet turned down so bravely, O
For to-night I shall sleep in a cold open field,
Along with the raggle taggle gypsies, O.

She Moved Through The Fair

Padraic Colum matched the elusive beauty of this traditional air with a poem of love lost and perhaps regained producing a seamless whole full of wistful enchantment.

My____ young love said to me my mother won't mind, And my father won't slight you for your lack of kine, And she stepped a-way from me and this she did say, It____ will not be long love till our wed-ding day.

She stepped away from me, and moved through the fair,
And sadly I watched her, move here and move there,
Then she went homeward with one star awake-
As the swan in the evening moves over the lake.

The people were saying no two were e'er wed,
But one had a sorrow that never was said,
She went away from me with her goods and her gear,
And that was the last that I saw of my dear.

Last night she came to me, my dear love came in,
So softly she came that her feet made no din,
She laid her hand on me, and this she did say:
'It will not be long, love, till our wedding day.'

"Esso and the Ass" on the Heath, near Portlaoise, 1938.

The Rocky Road to Dublin

The words are from a 19th century broadsheet and the air is a slip jig number 411 in O'Neills "Dance Music of Ireland".

In the mer-ry month of June from my home I star-ted

left the girls of Tuam near-ly bro-ken hear-ted, sa-

lu-ted fa-ther dear kissed my dar-lin' mo-ther

drank a pint of beer my grief and tears to smo-ther, then

off to reap the corn and leave where I was born, I

cut a stout black-thorn to ban-ish ghost and gob-lin, in a

brand new pair of brogues I ratt-led o'er the bogs, I

frigh-tened all the dogs on the rock-y road to Dub-lin.

Chorus

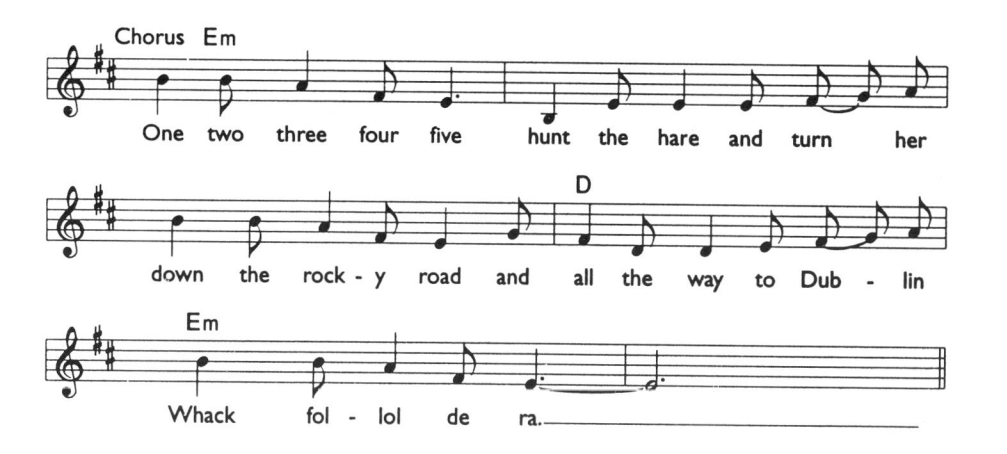

One two three four five hunt the hare and turn her down the rock-y road and all the way to Dub-lin Whack fol-lol de ra.

In Mullingar that night I rested limbs so weary,
Started by daylight next morning light and airy,
Took a drop of the pure, to keep my heart from sinking,
That's an Irishman's cure, whene'er he's on for drinking,
To see the lasses smile, laughing all the while,
At my curious style, 'twould set your heart a-bubbling,
They ax'd if I was hired, the wages I required,
Till I was almost tired of the rocky road to Dublin.

In Dublin next arrived, I thought it such a pity,
To be so soon deprived a view of that fine city,
Then I took a stroll among the quality,
My bundle it was stole in a neat locality:
Something crossed my mind, then I looked behind,
No bundle could I find upon me stick a-wobblin',
Enquiring for the rogue, they said my Connaught brogue,
Wasn't much in vogue on the rocky road to Dublin.

From there I got away my spirits never failing,
Landed on the quay as the ship was sailing,
Captain at me roared, said that no room had he,
When I jumped aboard, a cabin found for Paddy
Down among the pigs, I played some funny rigs
Danced some hearty jigs, the water round me bubblin'
When off to Holyhead I wished myself was dead,
Or better far, instead, on the rocky road to Dublin.

The boys of Liverpool, when we safely landed,
Called myself a fool, I could no longer stand it:
Blood began to boil, temper I was losin'
Poor old Erin's isle they began abusin'
'Hurrah my soul' sez I, me shillelagh I let fly,
Some Galway boys were by, saw I was a hobble in,
Then with a loud Hurrah, they joined in the affray,
We quickly cleared the way, for the rocky road to Dublin.